THE
FAMILY ALBUM
OF
BEATRIX POTTER

Published by Derrydale Books,
distributed by Random House Value Publishing, Inc.
40 Engelhard Avenue
Avenel, New Jersey 07001

Printed and bound in Singapore

Library of Congress Cataloging–in–Publication Data

ISBN 0–517–14729–7

8 7 6 5 4 3 2 1

THE
FAMILY ALBUM
OF
BEATRIX POTTER

Text by Abigail Jacobs

DERRYDALE BOOKS
NEW YORK • AVENEL

CONTENTS

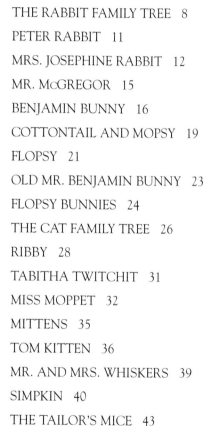

INTRODUCTION

As you turn the pages of this delightful new family album, you will meet all the lovable little creatures in the world of Beatrix Potter, beginning with everyone's favorite bunny, Peter Rabbit. All the characters in this book have their own adventures and their own stories. The youngsters are often helpful and brave, but they can be rascally, too. The mothers and fathers keep busy shopping, cleaning, and hosting dinner parties—and worrying a great deal about their children, who seem to get into considerable mischief.

Benjamin Bunny, for example, is a naughty little fellow—until he grows up and has children of his own. Tabitha Twitchit has her hands full managing a store and chasing after her three disobedient kittens. Jemima Puddle-duck trusts a foxy-whiskered fellow, then discovers that he is not as nice as he pretends to be. Among the others you will read about are sassy Squirrel Nutkin, fastidious Mrs. Tittlemouse, a pair of villainous rats, and a hedgehog who is a very exacting laundress.

Beatrix Potter got the ideas for her stories from her own household menagerie. As a child in London she was lonely and shy, and her only playmate was her younger brother, Bertram. Their stern parents rarely let them play outside, but on family vacations in the country, Beatrix and Bertram could run free. Beatrix befriended all kinds of animals—cats, mice, rabbits, snails, a tortoise, even a hedgehog—and she brought some of her pets back home to the city. With her extraordinary talent for drawing, she captured their funny antics and expressions in small sketches and watercolor paintings.

When Beatrix Potter grew up, she made up stories about her favorite animals, giving them human personalities and families and busy lives. Her stories became famous all around the world. In *The Family Album of Beatrix Potter* you will meet all of her furry friends; some are funny, others are wise, some are heroic, and some are not nice at all! So turn the page and let's have a peek at what they are up to. . . .

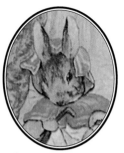 

Mrs. Josephine Rabbit married Father Rabbit

Black Rabbit married Cottontail   Peter

FAMILY TREE

Old Mr. Benjamin Bunny
"Bouncer"

Mopsy

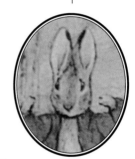

Flopsy married Benjamin Bunny

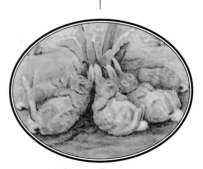

Flopsy Bunnies

PETER RABBIT

This is Peter Rabbit,
everybody's favorite bunny.
He is often very naughty
and doesn't listen to his
mother's warning to stay out
of Mr. McGregor's garden.
He risks his life and loses
his clothes, too. Is it worth it
just for some lettuce and
a few beans?

MRS. JOSEPHINE RABBIT

Mrs. Rabbit has raised her four
children all by herself—ever since
Mr. Rabbit was caught by
Mr. McGregor and made into a pie
by his wife. If only Peter were
more obedient, she would have
an easier time, for her three
daughters, Flopsy, Mopsy, and
Cottontail, are all good little bunnies.
Mrs. Rabbit has a shop where
she sells herbs, tea, and mittens
that she knits herself.

MR. McGREGOR

Mr. McGregor does not
want any rabbits hopping
through his garden and
stealing his vegetables.
But bunnies really don't eat
very much, after all.
Why can't Mr. McGregor
just leave them alone!

BENJAMIN BUNNY

Young Benjamin Bunny
swaggers bravely as he leads
his cousin Peter back into
Mr. McGregor's dangerous
garden. But at the sight of
a big black cat, Benjamin loses
his courage. He and Peter
have to hide from that cat for
five hours. But at least they
get what they came for—
Peter's lost clothes.

COTTONTAIL
AND MOPSY

Peter Rabbit's sisters always help their
mother and they love to pick berries.
When Cottontail grows up, she marries
a black bunny and they live with
their children on the hill.

As for Mopsy, no one has seen her in
many years. Do *you* know
where she might be?

FLOPSY

Flopsy is another of Peter Rabbit's
sisters. She marries her cousin
Benjamin Bunny and they
have lots of cute little
children, called the Flopsy
Bunnies. Poor Flopsy spends a
lot of her time worrying,
because her bunnies are
always getting themselves into
perilous situations.

OLD MR. BENJAMIN BUNNY

Old Mr. Bunny, whose
nickname is "Bouncer," thinks he
knows a lot about raising children.
When his son Benjamin and nephew
Peter Rabbit get into a jam,
Mr. Bunny rescues them.
But some years later, when
Bouncer babysits for his
grandchildren, the Flopsy
Bunnies, he doesn't do a very
good job at all. Those sweet
little bunnies get kidnapped
from right under his nose!

FLOPSY BUNNIES

The playful little Flopsy Bunnies
keep getting into really serious
danger. One day they are
squashed into a sack by
Mr. McGregor, who finds them
among the grass clippings in his
garden. Another time they are
kidnapped and trapped in an
oven by the sinister badger
Tommy Brock. Is someone going
to rescue those innocent young
bunnies before they get eaten?

THE CAT

Ribby

cousins

Tom Kitten

FAMILY TREE

Tabitha Twitchit

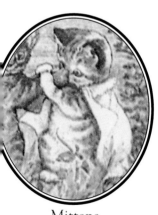

Mittens

Miss Moppet

RIBBY

Mrs. Ribston, known as Ribby,
is a take-charge kind of cat.
She does *not* approve of the misbehavior
of her cousin Tabitha Twitchit's
kittens, and she is *not* afraid of rats.
But when Ribby invites her friend
Duchess the dog for tea, she sets a
lovely table and cooks a scrumptious
mouse and bacon pie.

TABITHA TWITCHIT

This busy pussy cat has a
general store in the village and
is the mother of three
very rascally little kittens:
Tom, Miss Moppet, and Mittens.
Mrs. Twitchit is a nervous parent,
perhaps because she keeps
losing those kittens—and
whenever they run off
they get into mischief.

MISS MOPPET

Miss Moppet is always ready
to play. One day a sassy little
mouse peeps out of a cabinet and
makes fun of Miss Moppet.
That's not a nice way to treat
a kitten. So Miss Moppet decides
to tease that mouse right back.

MITTENS

As a kitten, Mittens enjoys a
good prank just as much as her
sister, Miss Moppet, and her
brother, Tom Kitten. But when Mittens
grows up, she joins Moppet in a very
successful rat-catching business.

TOM KITTEN

Chubby Tom Kitten seems to
attract trouble! What can his
mother, Tabitha Twitchit, do?
If she dresses him up for
company, he just makes a mess
of himself. If she locks him in
the cupboard to keep him safe
while she does her baking, he
sneaks out—and the next thing
he knows, he is being rolled in
dough to make a dumpling for
a couple of nasty old rats!

MR. AND MRS. WHISKERS

Old Mr. Whiskers is furious
when little Tom Kitten, who is
as dirty as a little cat can get,
tumbles right onto his bed.
Then Samuel has an idea, and
his mouth starts to water as he
and his wife, Anna Maria, decide to
make a delicious dinner—with
poor Tom as the main course.

SIMPKIN

This busy cat looks forward to a
delicious meal of mice at the end
of a long day. When his owner,
the tailor, lets Simpkin's dinner escape,
Simpkin is not only hungry—he's
looking for revenge!

THE TAILOR'S MICE

What will happen to the poor
tailor of Gloucester?
The mayor needs a new coat for
his wedding day, but the tailor is
sick in bed, tossing and turning
with fever. Who would ever
guess that the little brown mice
who live in the tailor's shop
could save the day with a
"snippeting of scissors, and
snappeting of thread"?

TOM THUMB AND HUNCA MUNCA

Tom Thumb and his wife,
Hunca Munca, squeak with joy
at the sight of all the tasty
dishes set out on the table in
the dollhouse. When they
discover that these foods are
not real, their happiness turns
quickly to rage. What a mess they
make! But nice mice do clean up, too.

JOHNNY TOWN-MOUSE

Johnny Town-mouse
enjoys nothing better than
an elegant dinner party in his
fancy city home. He thinks that
being chased by the house cat
is a small price to pay for
fine crumbs and fancy desserts.
A nice quiet life in the country
is too boring for Johnny!

TIMMY WILLIE

The city is a frightening place to a
sweet little country mouse like
Timmy Willie, who prefers his own
home in the peaceful countryside.
Timmy is as happy as can be
shelling corn and enjoying the
sweet fragrance of the wildflowers.

MRS. TITTLEMOUSE

Thomasina Tittlemouse keeps calm
in an emergency, which is lucky
for the Flopsy Bunnies when they
get into trouble. She's also a careful
housekeeper, although it's not
easy for a tidy little
woodmouse to keep a clean
home when messy visitors
keep dropping in.

OLD MR. BROWN

Inscrutable old Mr. Brown is
always serious and silent as he
accepts gifts from the squirrels
who gather nuts on Owl Island.
But Squirrel Nutkin's pranks
and rudeness just might be
testing the owl's patience.

SQUIRREL NUTKIN

Squirrel Nutkin likes to dance
and sing and ask riddles.
He can be terribly rude, and if he
doesn't watch out, he may get
skinned by old Mr. Brown.
An owl can take only so much
before he gets mad!

TWINKLEBERRY

Unlike his brother, Squirrel
Nutkin, Twinkleberry doesn't
fritter away his time in play.
He is much too busy gathering
nuts so he'll have something to
eat during the cold winter.

TIMMY AND GOODY TIPTOES

Prudent Timmy Tiptoes and his
wife, Goody, are busy squirreling
away nuts for the winter.
"Who's been digging up *my* nuts?"
taunt some other squirrels,
and in a twinkling they pounce upon
poor Timmy. What can this
innocent squirrel do?

JEMIMA PUDDLE-DUCK

Jemima Puddle-duck is silly
when she plays dress-up in other
people's clothes. But she is
always serious about her eggs.
One day Jemima decides to
outsmart the meddling farmer's
wife and hatch her own eggs.
Meanwhile, there's a "foxy-
whiskered gentleman" trying to
outsmart Jemima . . . do you
think a hungry fox really plans
to *help* Jemima?

KEP THE COLLIE

Kep the collie is not as naive
as Jemima Puddle-duck.
He knows better than to trust a
stranger with foxy whiskers,
no matter how polite he seems to be!
Jemima is lucky to have
such a smart friend.

DUCHESS

Duchess the dog is pleased to
be invited to tea at the home of
Ribby the cat. Still, Duchess
shudders at the thought of
eating mouse pie. So she tries
to take matters into her own
hands . . . but even the best-laid
plans can backfire!

GINGER AND PICKLES

At the village store owned by
Ginger the tomcat and
Pickles the terrier, all shopping is
done on credit—that is,
no money is ever collected
from the customers. But this does leave
the shopkeepers in a bit of
a financial pickle.

MRS. TIGGY-WINKLE

When old Mrs. Rabbit and Tom
Titmouse need their dirty clothes
washed and ironed, they bring them
to Mrs. Tiggy-winkle. She is
extremely good at getting out stains.
Indeed, this sweet little
washerwoman does the laundry
of everyone in the whole village.
Mrs. Tiggy-winkle is very nice, but why
is she so small and prickly? What sort
of a person is she?

MR. JACKSON

"Tiddly, widdly, widdly." Mr. Jackson smells honey. A fat toad with sloppy wet feet is not a welcome visitor, but Mrs. Tittlemouse tries to be polite. "Buzz, buzz!" Perhaps Mr. Jackson can be useful after all, for he is not afraid of bees—and Mrs. Tittlemouse does not want those pests in her home another minute.

MR. JEREMY FISHER

Dinner parties are fun.
"If I catch more than five fish,"
says Mr. Jeremy Fisher,
"I will invite my friends."
But his day does not go as planned—
and he is lucky his raincoat tastes
so unpleasant, or Mr. Jeremy
himself might have ended up
as someone's dinner!

MR. TOD

When Mr. Tod is in a foul mood, everyone else had better watch out. Certainly the rabbits know this. But how about that disagreeable Tommy Brock— can cunning Mr. Tod teach the badger a lesson, or has the wily fox finally met his match?

TOMMY BROCK

Nasty Tommy Brock has no
scruples and no regard for
anyone else's property. Why,
it wouldn't bother him one bit to
eat his friend's grandchildren
for breakfast or to
set up housekeeping in his
enemy's home. Don't you
think it's high time someone
put a stop to his selfish exploits?

AUNT PETTITOES

It's not easy being the mother
of eight mischievous little
piglings, but Aunt Pettitoes has
tried her best. At least she can
be proud of their big appetites.
Still, it's a tearful day when
she must send her children out
into the world. Do you think
they'll be all right on their own?

PIGLING BLAND
AND ALEXANDER

Pigling Bland and his brother
Alexander are on their way to
Market Town. Pigling Bland is a
well-behaved fellow, but Alexander acts
so silly that a policeman comes and
takes him home. Then Pigling Bland
gets quite lost. "Wee, wee, wee! I can't
find my way back home!" he cries.
But the next day he finds love
in a most unexpected place.

PIG-WIG

Surely this lovely little black Berkshire
pig deserves more than to become bacon
and ham for the thieving farmer who
stole her. Please, won't someone rescue
Pig-wig from this sad fate?

BEATRIX POTTER

Beatrix Potter drew all the pictures
in this book, and created all these
characters—and then she climbed
right onto some of the pages!
Here she is, watching Samuel and
Anna Maria Whiskers borrow her
wheelbarrow—without permission.
Another day she helps Pigling
Bland and Alexander get ready for
their trip to market.

WHERE TO FIND YOUR FAVORITE
CHARACTERS IN BEATRIX POTTER'S BOOKS

Peter Rabbit .... *The Tale of Peter Rabbit*
The Tale of Benjamin Bunny
The Tale of the Flopsy Bunnies
The Tale of Mrs. Tiggy-Winkle
The Tale of Mr. Tod

Mrs. Josephine Rabbit .... *The Tale of Peter Rabbit*
The Tale of Benjamin Bunny
The Tale of Mrs. Tiggy-Winkle

Mr. McGregor .... *The Tale of Peter Rabbit*
The Tale of Benjamin Bunny
The Tale of the Flopsy Bunnies

Benjamin Bunny .... *The Tale of Benjamin Bunny*
The Tale of the Flopsy Bunnies
The Tale of Mr. Tod
The Tale of Mrs. Tiggy-Winkle

Flopsy .... *The Tale of Peter Rabbit*
The Tale of Benjamin Bunny
The Tale of the Flopsy Bunnies
The Tale of Mr. Tod

Mopsy .... *The Tale of Peter Rabbit*
The Tale of Benjamin Bunny

Cottontail .... *The Tale of Peter Rabbit*
The Tale of Benjamin Bunny
The Tale of Mr. Tod
Appley Dapsley's Nursery Rhymes